上海市中高职贯通教育

英语课程标准

(试行稿)

上海市教育委员会教学研究室 编

华东师范大学出版社
·上海·

图书在版编目（CIP）数据

上海市中高职贯通教育英语课程标准：试行稿／上海市教育委员会教学研究室编．—上海：华东师范大学出版社，2022
 ISBN 978-7-5760-3447-9

Ⅰ.①上… Ⅱ.①上… Ⅲ.①英语-课程标准-职业教育 Ⅳ.①H319.3

中国版本图书馆 CIP 数据核字(2022)第 223643 号

上海市中高职贯通教育英语课程标准（试行稿）

编　　者	上海市教育委员会教学研究室
责任编辑	蒋梦婷
审读编辑	袁一遘
责任校对	郭　红
装帧设计	庄玉侠
出版发行	华东师范大学出版社
社　　址	上海市中山北路 3663 号　邮编 200062
网　　址	www.ecnupress.com.cn
电　　话	021-60821666　行政传真 021-62572105
客服电话	021-62865537　门市(邮购)电话 021-62869887
地　　址	上海市中山北路 3663 号华东师范大学校内先锋路口
网　　店	http://hdsdcbs.tmall.com
印　刷　者	常熟市文化印刷有限公司
开　　本	787 毫米×1092 毫米　1/16
印　　张	7
字　　数	88 千字
版　　次	2023 年 1 月第 1 版
印　　次	2023 年 1 月第 1 次
书　　号	ISBN 978-7-5760-3447-9
定　　价	99.40 元

出版人　王　焰

(如发现本版图书有印订质量问题，请寄回本社客服中心调换或电话 021-62865537 联系)

上海市教育委员会文件

沪教委职〔2022〕41号

上海市教育委员会关于印发上海市中高职贯通教育数学等3门公共基础课程标准（试行稿）的通知

各有关高等学校，各区教育局，各有关委、局、控股（集团）公司：

  为贯彻落实《国家职业教育改革实施方案》《推进现代职业教育高质量发展的意见》《上海市教育发展"十四五"规划》等精神，进一步完善上海现代职业教育体系建设，市教委制定了《上海市中高职贯通教育数学课程标准（试行稿）》《上海市中高职贯通教育英语课程标准（试行稿）》和《上海市中高职贯通教育信息技术课程标准（试行稿）》（以下简称《课程标准》），现印发给你们，请从2022年秋季招收的中高职贯通、五年一贯制新生起组织实施。

上述3门《课程标准》是规范本市中高职贯通和五年一贯制专业数学、英语和信息技术基础等公共基础课程教学的指导性文件，是学校组织教学工作，检查教学质量，评价教学效果，选编教材和配备教学设施设备的依据。各相关职业学校主管部门和直属单位、教科研机构（组织）等要根据《课程标准》，加强对学校专业教学工作的指导。附件请至上海教育网站 http://edu.sh.gov.cn/下载。

附件：1.上海市中高职贯通教育数学课程标准（试行稿）

2.上海市中高职贯通教育英语课程标准（试行稿）

3.上海市中高职贯通教育信息技术课程标准（试行稿）

上海市教育委员会

2022年10月20日

抄送：各中等职业学校，各有关直属事业单位。

上海市教育委员会办公室　　　　　　　　2022年10月24日印发

目 录

一、导言 /1
 （一）课程定位 /1
 （二）课程理念 /1

二、学科核心素养 /3
 （一）职场语言能力 /3
 （二）跨文化能力 /3
 （三）学习能力 /4

三、课程目标 /5
 （一）职场语言运用能力目标 /5
 （二）跨文化理解能力目标 /5
 （三）可持续学习能力目标 /5

四、课程结构 /6

五、课程内容与要求 /7
 （一）语言技能 /7
 （二）语言知识 /12

（三）文化知识 /17

六、学业质量 /18

（一）学业质量内涵 /18

（二）学业质量水平描述 /18

七、实施建议 /20

（一）教材编写 /20

（二）教学实施 /21

（三）学习评价 /26

（四）资源建设 /27

（五）保障措施 /28

附 录 /30

附录1：交际功能项目表 /30

附录2：话题 /32

附录3：词汇表 /33

附录4：中华优秀传统文化常用词汇 /94

上海市中高职贯通教育英语课程标准开发项目组名单 /101

参考文献 /103

一、导言

（一）课程定位

英语是思想文化的重要载体和国际交流的主要工具。英语学习有助于推动对外交往和服务社会经济，在满足职业院校学生的生活和职场需求，促进其生涯发展方面也起着不可低估的作用。

中高职贯通教育英语课程是中高职贯通和五年一贯制学生的一门必修公共基础课程，是中高职贯通培养课程体系的重要组成部分，具有很强的实践性与应用性。

中高职贯通教育英语课程在党的教育方针指引下，以职业发展为导向，聚焦语言实践，帮助学生拓展国际视野、增强文化自信、厚植家国情怀，进而全面提升学生的学科核心素养，使其成为德技兼备的高素质技术技能人才。

（二）课程理念

中高职贯通教育英语课程须全面贯彻党的教育方针，以社会主义核心价值观为统领，根据党和国家对教育的要求，落实立德树人根本任务。同时，课程应体现职业教育类型特征，遵循长学制不同学习阶段学生的身心发展规律和教育教学规律，准确把握中高职贯通教育人才培养的定位，基于初中毕业起点、高职专科层次规格的学生发展实际需求，对教学内容和要求进行系统规划和一体化设计，呈现螺旋递进、逐级上升的特点。具体理念体现如下：

1. 聚焦语言能力，提升核心素养

本课程聚焦语言运用能力，以能力培养带动知识学习，并促进情感、态度和价值观

提升,旨在发展学生的职场语言能力、跨文化能力和学习能力等学科核心素养。

2. 凸显职业特色,服务生涯发展

以职业发展为导向,突出职场语言运用能力的培养。提供具有职业特色的学习内容与学习活动,服务学生的专业学习。根据具体专业的需要,在语言能力培养方面有所侧重,为专业英语学习和职场语言运用创造条件,从而为学生的就业和生涯发展奠定基础。

3. 倡导知行合一,强化语言实践

改变以语言知识为中心的教学模式,以核心素养为引领,创设生活和职场情境,基于意义开展语言活动,同时有机融入语言知识的学习,从而推动学生主动参与语言实践,提升其语言运用能力。

4. 实施多元评价,推动教学变革

推进评价内容、评价方式与评价主体等的多元化。基于核心素养,确定核心内容。在实施终结性评价的基础上,充分重视过程性评价,尝试开展增值性评价和表现性评价。除了教师和专业性评价机构外,学生、学校、行业等均可参与评价。同时针对学生不同的学习基础开展分层评价,逐步形成立体评价体系,充分发挥评价的激励作用,以多元评价推动教与学的根本转变。

5. 运用数字技术,促进有效学习

重视数字技术与课程的融合,营造有效教学环境,丰富课程资源,拓展学习渠道;运用数字技术实施差异教学,以适应学生不同的学习基础,满足不同的个性发展和职业发展需求;借助数字技术落实精准评价,促进学生的有效学习,推动英语学科核心素养的形成与发展。

二、学科核心素养

学科核心素养是学科育人价值的集中体现,是学生通过学习逐步形成的、能够适应终身发展和社会发展需要的正确价值观、必备品格和关键能力。中高职贯通教育英语学科核心素养主要包括职场语言能力、跨文化能力和学习能力。它们之间呈现相互渗透、融合互动、共同发展的协同关系。

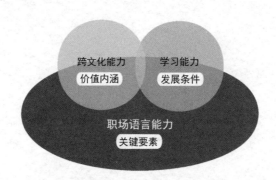

图 1 中高职贯通教育英语学科核心素养示意图

(一) 职场语言能力

职场语言能力是指学生通过本课程的学习,掌握基本的语言知识和语言技能,在生活和职场情境中能有效、得体地进行口头交流与书面沟通。职场语言能力是中高职贯通教育英语学科核心素养的关键要素,为学生的职业发展奠定基础。

(二) 跨文化能力

跨文化能力是指学生通过对中外优秀文化的感知与理解,掌握文化知识,秉持开放、包容与合作的精神,形成跨文化交际意识,实现有效的沟通与交流,坚定文化自信。

跨文化能力构成中高职贯通教育英语学科核心素养的价值内涵，有助于学生正确价值观的形成。

（三）学习能力

学习能力是指学生积极利用英语学习资源，主动调适学习策略，养成良好的学习习惯，提升思维品质，提高学习效率。学习能力为中高职贯通教育英语学科核心素养的发展创造条件，有利于学生的可持续发展。

三、课程目标

中高职贯通教育英语课程应全面贯彻党的教育方针,培育和践行社会主义核心价值观,落实立德树人根本任务。在义务教育的基础上,通过五年长学制培养,进一步促进学生学科核心素养的可持续发展,使其达到高职专科层次的英语水平要求,成为具有家国情怀、国际视野和英语沟通能力的高素质技术技能人才。

中高职贯通教育英语课程旨在培养和发展学生的职场语言能力、跨文化能力和学习能力等学科核心素养。通过本课程的学习,学生应能达成基于本学科核心素养制定的课程目标。

(一)职场语言运用能力目标

能够综合运用所学的英语语言知识、语言技能和交际策略,基于生活和职场情境,比较准确地理解信息、传递观点,表达情感与态度,积累语言经验,恰当、有效地进行交流与沟通。

(二)跨文化理解能力目标

能够理解与尊重中外不同文化背景下思维方式的差异,认同与借鉴国外优秀文化,发展同理心,并能换位思考;坚持民族自尊,坚定文化自信,能够用英语讲好中国故事,促进中华优秀文化传播。

(三)可持续学习能力目标

能够具有持续的学习动机、兴趣和良好的学习习惯,利用多种学习资源与学习策略,不断反思与优化学习方法与过程,改善思维品质,进而提升可持续学习意识和能力。

四、课程结构

中高职贯通教育英语课程应凸显中高职有机衔接和一体化设计的特点。学生主要学习基础模块和拓展模块,其中拓展模块包含拓展模块一(基础拓展)和拓展模块二(职业提升)两个部分。

基础模块是为学生继续学习与职业发展奠定基础的课程,拓展模块一(基础拓展)是满足学生继续学习需求的基础拓展课程,拓展模块二(职业提升)是服务学生未来生涯发展的职业提升课程。

课程必修总学时数为288学时,对应基础模块,计16学分。课程选修总学时数为144学时,其中拓展模块一(基础拓展)占108学时,计6学分;拓展模块二(职业提升)占36学时,计2学分。

表1 中高职贯通教育英语课程结构

模块	性质	学时	学分
基础	必修	288	16
拓展一(基础拓展)	选修	108	6
拓展二(职业提升)	选修	36	2

基础模块的总学时为288学时,建议其中216学时在前6学期开设,72学时在后4学期开设。拓展模块的总学时为144学时,在基础模块课程开设的前提下,学校可根据专业实际需要和学生发展需求,确定合适的学期,自主选择开设相应的拓展模块,并保持课程安排、教学内容的连贯性。

五、课程内容与要求

中高职贯通教育英语课程内容应有机融入思政元素,落实立德树人根本任务,指向英语学科核心素养,注重语言实践与应用。具体内容涵盖语言技能、语言知识和文化知识,其中语言技能包含视听、口语、阅读、写作和翻译五种技能,语言知识包含语音、词汇、语法、语篇和语用五个部分,文化知识则包含文化信息和文化内涵两项内容。

在中高职贯通教育英语课程的基础模块和拓展模块一(基础拓展)学习阶段,学生的语言技能、语言知识和文化知识分别达到基本和较高两个等级要求,学生能进行有效的职场沟通与交流,具备一定的跨文化理解能力和可持续学习能力。

由于不同专业对拓展模块二(职业提升)的需求差异较大,本标准对该模块的学习内容与要求不作统一规定,各校可根据实际情况,自行确定相应的学习内容与要求。

(一)语言技能

1. 视听技能

表2 视听技能的表现、描述与学习要求

技能表现	技能描述	学习要求	
		基本	较高
1. 获取事实信息	1-1 能从话题熟悉、语速较慢且与生活和职场相关的简单视听语料中获取主要事实信息	√	

续 表

技能表现	技能描述	学习要求 基本	学习要求 较高
1. 获取事实信息	1-2 能从话题常见、语速适中且与生活和职场相关的视听语料中获取主要事实信息和关键细节信息	√	
	1-3 能从语速正常、语言较为复杂且与职场相关的视听语料中获取主要事实信息和关键细节信息		√
2. 理解主旨与归纳大意	2-1 能辨别与生活和职场相关的简单视听语料的话题	√	
	2-2 能概括话题常见、语速适中且与生活和职场相关的视听语料的主要内容及观点	√	
	2-3 能概括语速正常、语言较为复杂且与职场相关的视听语料的主要内容及观点		√
3. 推断隐含意义	3-1 能从与生活和职场相关的简短对话中推断说话者的意图	√	
	3-2 能从话题常见、语速适中且与生活和职场相关的视听语料中领会说话者的情感态度，并辨别其立场	√	
	3-3 能从语速正常、语言较为复杂且与职场相关的视听语料中推断说话者的言外之意		√

学习经历及情感态度要求：
　　学生在视听活动中，借助教科书、音频、视频及网络平台等资源，运用视听策略，感受语音、语调、词汇、文化知识等在具体情境中的实际运用，体验视听学习的过程，养成良好的视听习惯和积极的视听态度，增强对英语视听学习的兴趣和信心，提高视听能力。

2. 口语技能

表3 口语技能的表现、描述与学习要求

技能表现	技能描述	学习要求 基本	学习要求 较高
1. 朗读	1-1 能模仿音频、视频中标准的语音、语调	√	
	1-2 能运用正确的语音、语调朗读，在朗读中正确运用意群、重读、弱读、连读、失去爆破和浊化等语音技巧	√	

续 表

技 能 表 现	技 能 描 述	学习要求 基本	学习要求 较高
1.朗读	1-3 能运用正确的语音、语调朗读,在朗读中反映出不同语调、节奏等语音特征所传达的意义和说话者所表达的意图		√
2.表达	2-1 能简单复述短文大意或转述他人传达的信息	√	
2.表达	2-2 能借助提示,就熟悉的话题对人物和事件等进行简单描述,并简要表达自己的观点	√	
2.表达	2-3 能就生活和职场中常见的话题表达自己的观点		√
3.交流	3-1 能对日常话语作出较为恰当的应答	√	
3.交流	3-2 能用简单的提问获取重要信息	√	
3.交流	3-3 能就生活和职场中的熟悉话题与他人进行交流,并适时作出恰当回应		√

学习经历及情感态度要求:
　　学生在口语活动中,借助教科书、音频、视频及网络平台等资源,运用口语学习策略和跨文化交际策略在生活和职场情境中进行口语实践,克服羞怯心理,体验口语表达的过程,培养跨文化交际意识和主动使用英语进行交际的习惯,提升英语口语交际能力。

3. 阅读技能

表4　阅读技能的表现、描述与学习要求

技 能 表 现	技 能 描 述	学习要求 基本	学习要求 较高
1.获取事实信息	1-1 能从难度适中且与生活和职场相关的阅读语料中获取主要事实信息和关键细节信息	√	
1.获取事实信息	1-2 能从语言较为复杂且与职场相关的阅读语料中获取主要事实信息和关键细节信息		√
2.理解主旨与归纳大意	2-1 能理解和归纳难度适中且与生活和职场相关的阅读语料的段落大意和主旨大意	√	

续 表

技能表现	技能描述	学习要求 基本	学习要求 较高
2. 理解主旨与归纳大意	2-2 能理解和归纳语言较为复杂的职场阅读语料的段落大意和主旨大意		√
3. 推断隐含意义	3-1 能从与生活和职场相关的简单阅读语料中推断隐含的事实信息	√	
	3-2 能从难度适中且与生活和职场相关的阅读语料中推断隐含的观点和态度	√	
	3-3 能从语言较为复杂的职场阅读语料中推断隐含的观点与态度		√

学习经历及情感态度要求：
　　学生在阅读活动中，借助教科书、工具书和网络平台等资源，运用各种语言知识和基本的阅读策略增进对包含生活和职场情境的阅读语料(含非连续文本)及其文化背景的理解，增强英语阅读兴趣，养成良好的英语阅读习惯，提升思维品质，培养感受、理解、鉴赏与评价能力，提高英语阅读能力。

4. 写作技能

表5　写作技能的表现、描述与学习要求

技能表现	技能描述	学习要求 基本	学习要求 较高
1. 撰写常见的应用文	1-1 能填写履历表、申请表、产品报修单等生活和职场常用的表格	√	
	1-2 能撰写求职信、请假条、通知等简单的应用文	√	
	1-3 能撰写商务信函、活动方案、操作指南等较为复杂的职场应用文		√
2. 撰写简单的记叙文	2-1 能叙述简单的生活与职场事件等	√	
	2-2 能叙述熟悉的人或物的变化以及个人生活与工作经历等	√	
	2-3 能较有条理地完整叙述职场事件等		√

续 表

技能表现	技能描述	学习要求 基本	学习要求 较高
3. 撰写简单的说明文	3-1 能简要说明所熟悉产品的特点和用途等	√	
	3-2 能较为清晰地说明所熟悉岗位的基本工作流程或步骤等	√	
	3-3 能比较完整、清晰地解释或说明所熟悉的职场岗位要求等		√
4. 撰写简单的议论文	4-1 能使用简单的语言,就熟悉的话题提出观点,并简要提供理由	√	
	4-2 能就熟悉的话题表达观点,并使用一定的证据支撑观点	√	
	4-3 能就职场问题阐述观点,有论点和论据,具有较强的说服力		√

学习经历及情感态度要求:
　　学生在写作活动中,借助工具书和网络平台等资源,运用基本的语言知识和写作策略,通过有指导的写作实践,体会词法、句法和文化知识的运用,逐步克服畏惧写作的心理,完成简单的记叙文、说明文和议论文等文体的写作,提高书面表达能力。

5. 翻译技能

表 6　翻译技能的表现、描述与学习要求

技能表现	技能描述	学习要求 基本	学习要求 较高
1. 翻译常见类型的句子	1-1 能口头和书面翻译简单句	√	
	1-2 能口头和书面翻译难度适中的并列句和复合句	√	
	1-3 能口头和书面翻译较为复杂的句子		√
2. 翻译常见的指示性、交流性和说明性文本	2-1 能书面翻译标识语、活动日程等常见的指示性文本	√	
	2-2 能书面翻译求职信、推荐信、正式邀请函等常见的交流性文本	√	
	2-3 能书面翻译产品使用说明、事故处理报告等职场常见的说明性文本		√

续　表

技　能　表　现	技　能　描　述	学习要求 基本	学习要求 较高
3. 翻译常见的叙述性文本	3-1　能书面翻译难度适中的生活故事	√	
	3-2　能书面翻译难度适中的职场故事	√	
	3-3　能书面翻译较为复杂的职场叙述性文本		√

学习经历及情感态度要求：
　　学生在翻译活动中，借助工具书、翻译软件和网络平台等资源，运用基本的语言知识和翻译策略，通过有指导的翻译实践，体会语言知识和文化知识等的运用，逐步克服畏惧翻译的心理，完成常见指示性文本、交流性文本、说明性文本和叙述性文本的翻译，提高英汉互译的能力。

（二）语言知识

1. 语音知识

表7　语音知识的学习内容与要求

语言知识		知　识　描　述	学习要求 基本	学习要求 较高
语音	1. 基本语音	1-1　国际音标的发音	√	
		1-2　单词的读音	√	
	2. 读音规则	2-1　重读、弱读、连读、失去爆破、浊化、同化等	√	
		2-2　语调、节奏、停顿、意群、韵律等	√	
	3. 语音功能	3-1　根据重音、语调、节奏等变化感知说话人的意图和态度等	√	
		3-2　运用重音、语调、节奏等变化表达意义、意图和态度等		√

2. 词汇知识

表 8 词汇知识的学习内容与要求

语言知识		知 识 描 述	学习要求	
			基本	较高
词汇	1. 词汇量	1-1 基础模块学习阶段累计掌握词汇 2600 余个	√	
		1-2 在基础模块词汇量的基础上，拓展模块一（基础拓展）学习阶段累计掌握词汇 3100 余个，对拓展模块二（职业提升）学习阶段的词汇量不作统一规定		√
	2. 词义与用法	2-1 常用词汇与习惯搭配的意义	√	
		2-2 常用词汇与习惯搭配的用法	√	
		2-3 词汇使用的丰富性		√

3. 语法知识

表 9 语法知识的学习内容与要求

语言知识			知 识 描 述	学习要求	
				基本	较高
语法	1. 词法	1-1 名词	1-1-1 可数名词和不可数名词	√	
			1-1-2 专有名词	√	
			1-1-3 名词所有格	√	
		1-2 形容词	形容词及其比较级和最高级	√	
		1-3 副词	副词及其比较级和最高级	√	
		1-4 代词	人称代词、物主代词、反身代词、指示代词、不定代词、疑问代词、关系代词、连接代词	√	
		1-5 数词	1-5-1 基数词和序数词	√	

续 表

语言知识		知 识 描 述		学习要求	
				基本	较高
语法	1. 词法	1-5 数词	1-5-2 小数、分数、百分数	√	
		1-6 介词		√	
		1-7 连词		√	
		1-8 冠词		√	
		1-9 感叹词		√	
		1-10 动词	1-10-1 动词的基本形式、及物动词和不及物动词	√	
			1-10-2 系动词、助动词、情态动词	√	
			1-10-3 时态	1-10-3-1 一般现在时、一般过去时、一般将来时、现在进行时、过去进行时、现在完成时、过去完成时、过去将来时	√	
				1-10-3-2 将来进行时、将来完成时、现在完成进行时		√
			1-10-4 被动语态	1-10-4-1 一般现在时、一般过去时、一般将来时、现在进行时、现在完成时的被动语态	√	
				1-10-4-2 过去进行时、过去完成时的被动语态		√
			1-10-5 非谓语动词	1-10-5-1 动词不定式作宾语、补语	√	
				1-10-5-2 动词不定式作状语、定语	√	
				1-10-5-3 动词不定式作主语、表语	√	

续 表

语言知识			知 识 描 述		学习要求	
					基本	较高
语法	1. 词法	1-10 动词	1-10-5 非谓语动词	1-10-5-4 动词的-ing 形式作定语、状语、补语	√	
				1-10-5-5 动词的-ing 形式作主语、宾语、表语	√	
				1-10-5-6 动词的-ed 形式作定语、状语、补语	√	
				1-10-5-7 动词的-ed 形式作表语	√	
		1-11 构词法	合成法、派生法、转化法、缩写和简写		√	
	2. 句法	2-1 句子种类	陈述句、疑问句、祈使句、感叹句		√	
		2-2 句子成分	主语、谓语、宾语、补语、状语、表语、定语		√	
		2-3 基本句型	主语+谓语 主语+系动词+表语 主语+谓语+宾语 主语+谓语+间接宾语+直接宾语 主语+谓语+宾语+补语		√	
		2-4 主谓一致			√	
		2-5 独立主格结构				√
		2-6 并列句			√	
		2-7 复合句	2-7-1 名词性从句	2-7-1-1 宾语从句、主语从句、表语从句	√	
				2-7-1-2 同位语从句		√
			2-7-2 状语从句	2-7-2-1 时间状语从句、原因状语从句、条件状语从句、目的状语从句、让步状语从句、地点状语从句、结果状语从句	√	
				2-7-2-2 方式状语从句		√

续　表

语言知识		知　识　描　述		学习要求	
				基本	较高
语法	2.句法	2-7 复合句	2-7-3 定语从句	2-7-3-1 限制性定语从句	√	
				2-7-3-2 非限制性定语从句	√	
		2-8 特殊句式	2-8-1 存在句	√	
			2-8-2 省略句、倒装句、强调句		√
		2-9 虚拟语气			√

4.语篇知识

表 10　语篇知识的学习内容与要求

语言知识		知　识　描　述		学习要求	
				基本	较高
语篇	1.语篇类型	1-1	常见应用文的基本格式、基本结构及语言特点	√	
		1-2	记叙文和说明文的主要语篇特征	√	
		1-3	议论文的主要语篇特征和论证方法		√
	2.语篇结构	2-1	主题句、过渡句的作用、位置及行文特征	√	
		2-2	语篇中不同信息的组织方式	√	
		2-3	语篇成分之间的语义逻辑关系：次序关系、因果关系、概括与例证关系等		√
	3.衔接与连贯	3-1	语篇中的显性衔接和连贯手段	√	
		3-2	语篇中的隐性衔接和连贯手段		√

5. 语用知识

表 11　语用知识的学习内容与要求

语言知识	知　识　描　述		学习要求	
			基本	较高
语用	1. 功能知识	1-1　熟悉话题中基本的交际功能项目的表达方式	√	
		1-2　常见话题中多种交际功能项目的表达方式	√	
		1-3　社交场合中较为丰富的交际功能项目的表达方式		√
	2. 社会语言知识	2-1　一般社交场合中的礼貌用语及其文化规约	√	
		2-2　一般社交场合中礼节性用语的使用规范以及正式和非正式用语的区别	√	
		2-3　一般社交场合中语音、语调、音量、语速、节奏等的表达效果		√

（三）文化知识

表 12　文化知识的学习内容与要求

文化知识	知　识　描　述		学习要求	
			基本	较高
文化知识	1. 文化信息	1-1　中国和英语国家主要传统节日、风俗习惯、体育运动等	√	
		1-2　中国和英语国家主要文学家、艺术家、科学家的生平及其贡献等	√	
		1-3　世界重要历史文化现象和英语国家概况等		√
	2. 文化内涵	2-1　基本文化词汇的内涵	√	
		2-2　语篇中包含或反映的常见文化现象所蕴含的意义	√	
		2-3　中国与英语国家在风俗习惯或思维方式等方面的基本差异		√

六、学业质量

（一）学业质量内涵

学业质量是指学生完成本课程学习后的学业成就表现，是以学科核心素养及其能力目标为主要维度，根据基础模块和拓展模块一（基础拓展）的课程内容，对学生在生活和职场情境中运用英语沟通交流与完成任务的能力及表现的描述，是英语教学评价的基准。

（二）学业质量水平描述

本课程学业质量分为两个水平，分别对应"课程内容与要求"中的两个等级——基本和较高要求。水平一是学生在完成基础模块学习后应达到的基本要求，水平二是学生学习拓展模块一（基础拓展）后应达到的较高要求。由于不同学校的专业差异较大，拓展模块二（职业提升）的课程内容与学习要求不尽相同，对于该模块的学业质量水平不作统一规定。各学校可根据实际情况，自行制定相应的学业质量水平要求，对学生进行考核。

表 13　学业质量水平描述

质量水平	质量描述
水平一	1. 能识别包含常见生活和职场情境的语篇中的基本事实信息；能理解简单语篇的主旨、意义和情感；能识别简单的语言表达方式、常见的语篇结构和逻辑关系；能区分语篇中的事实和观点、证据和结论；能对语篇中的信息进行归类；能根据语篇中的信息作出基本的逻辑推断。

续 表

质量水平	质 量 描 述
水平一	2. 能以口头或书面形式陈述简单的事实,简要表达观点、态度等;能根据给定的信息,就生活和职场常见话题进行基本的交流;能就生活和职场中熟悉的话题和内容进行简单的中英互译;能用简单的英语写出常用的职场应用文。 3. 能理解简单语篇所包含的文化信息;能对语篇中不同的文化现象进行简单的比较,并理解中外基本的文化差异;能用简单的英语介绍中华优秀文化。 4. 能认识到英语学习的重要性;能确立较为明确的学习目标;能在学习中运用较为有效的学习策略和方法;能利用技术和渠道获取一定的学习资源;能形成自主学习的意识;能对自己的学习进行简单评价和反思。
水平二	1. 能识别包含较为复杂的生活和职场情境的语篇中的事实信息,理解语篇中的隐含信息;能理解语篇传递的主旨、意义和情感;能识别较为复杂的语言表达方式、篇章结构和逻辑关系;能对语篇中的信息进行归类和总结;能根据语篇中的信息作出恰当的逻辑推断。 2. 能就生活和职场中的相关话题与他人进行交流;能综合运用语言知识和资源,就相关职场话题进行有效沟通;能就生活和职场中的相关话题和内容进行中英互译;能用较为丰富的语言写出常见的职场应用文。 3. 能理解较为复杂的语篇所包含的文化信息;能识别与尊重较为复杂的语篇所包含的中外文化差异;能较为详细地介绍职场文化;能用较为丰富的语言介绍中华优秀文化。 4. 能正确认识英语学习的意义;能确立明确的学习目标;能制订合理的学习计划;能在学习中有效地运用学习策略和方法;能较为自主地利用多种技术与渠道获取丰富的学习资源;能形成自主学习的习惯与能力;能对自己的学习进行有效监控、评价与反思。

七、实施建议

中高职贯通教育英语课程实施应将思政教育融入全过程,以学科核心素养为指引,基于课程目标和课程内容,聚焦教材编写、教学实施、学习评价、资源建设、保障措施等。

(一) 教材编写

中高职贯通教育英语教材应以党的教育方针为指导,严格贯彻国家以及本市关于职业院校教材管理等相关文件精神,依据本课程标准中的课程定位、课程理念、学科核心素养、课程目标、课程结构、课程内容与要求等进行一体化编写,落实立德树人的根本任务。主要编写原则如下:

1. 全面落实立德树人,聚焦学科核心素养

中高职贯通教育英语教材的编写理念和设计思路应突出英语学科的育人价值,聚焦学科核心素养,将价值塑造、知识传授和能力培养融为一体,选定的教材内容和相应的活动设计应有利于学生树立正确的人生观、价值观和职业观,提升职场语言能力、跨文化能力和学习能力。

2. 依据英语课程标准,整体构建教材体系

中高职贯通教育英语教材应依据本课程标准进行编写,教材体系设计应基于学科核心素养,与课程目标保持一致,循序渐进,重点培养学生的职场语言运用能力、跨文化理解能力和可持续学习能力。应积极开发新形态教材,形成多模态、立体化的教材体系,充分满足学生的个性、兴趣和专业学习需求,为学生未来的职业发展和终身学习奠定基础。

3. 体现职业教育特色,合理编排教材内容

中高职贯通教育英语教材所选择的语料需涵盖生活和职场中的典型语篇类型,应

使用真实、地道和得体的语言,反映英语语言和中外优秀文化的多样性,体现当代社会生活、科技进步和职场发展等方面的内容。教材内容的编排应融合国际先进职业教育理念,对接学生的专业学习,遵循实践导向的设计思路,强调用英语开展具有职场特征的活动,实现职场沟通与交流,帮助学生提升职场语言沟通能力,发展高阶思维,凸显职业教育特色。

4. 深度融合数字技术,开发教材配套资源

中高职贯通教育英语教材应遵循学生语言学习规律和认知特点,深度融合数字技术,利用网络学习平台和学习软件等助力构建真实、开放、交互、合作的教学环境,引导学生开展自主与合作学习,加强学习体验;利用数字技术,丰富教材配套资源,包括学习的工具、途径、方法与策略等,推动有效学习,促进核心素养的整体提升,优化中高职贯通教育英语课程实施。

5. 优化编写团队结构,保障教材编写质量

教材编写人员需要政治立场坚定,熟悉教育教学规律和学生身心发展规律,在英语教材编写以及教科研方面有较高造诣,熟悉相关行业发展前沿的知识与技术。教材编写团队应包含学科领域专家、中高职教科研人员、中高职一线骨干教师以及行业企业的专家等。教材编写过程中应该多方征求意见,邀请教学以及行业专家审核,并根据专家审核意见进行完善,保障教材编写质量。

(二)教学实施

中高职贯通教育英语教学实施应基于立德树人根本任务,在学科核心素养的引领下,逐步落实课程目标,真正促进学生发展。具体遵循下列原则与建议:

1. 总体原则

(1)聚焦核心素养,落实立德树人

中高职贯通教育英语教学应聚焦学科核心素养,依照核心素养内涵和课程目标要求,在遵循英语教学规律和适应职业院校学生英语学习特点的基础上,制定教学目标,选择合适的教学内容,创设较为真实的英语使用情境,开展形式多样的学习活动,促进教学目标的达成,从而全面提升学生的英语学科核心素养,切实完成立德树人的根本任务。

(2) 凸显学科特点,注重语言交际

在中高职贯通教育英语教学一体化设计与实施过程中,应遵循语言学习规律,知识、技能等学习内容的安排需相互衔接、由易到难、适度复现,并力求语言形式与意义之间的平衡。同时,中高职贯通教育英语教学应考虑未来职场对职业院校技术技能人才的培养需求,重视学生听说能力的培养,切实推动其职场语言运用能力的提升。在进行基础知识教学和基本技能训练的同时,应努力创设生活和职场情境,帮助学生基于信息差、意见差和推理差等进行语言交际,用语言做事,充分发挥语言的交际功能,增强学生的语言交际能力。

(3) 利用数字技术,推动学习变革

教师应主动适应科技革命带来的英语教学理念和学生学习方式的变革,加强学习,不断提高自身的数字技术应用水平,将数字技术与英语教学深度融合,改进教学方法和教学评价,利用和开发各种教学资源,努力构建真实、开放、交互、合作的线上线下混合学习环境,拓展英语学习空间,大幅提高英语教学效率,优化学生学习效果。

(4) 兼顾学生差异,满足不同需求

中高职贯通教育英语教学应基于学生在学习基础、学习习惯、学习方法、所学专业等各方面存在的客观差异,既要关注全体学生的整体培养要求,又要尊重学生的个体差异与需求,本着"因材施教"的原则,聚焦内容、过程与产出,努力构建差异化教学模式。同时适当引入跨学科学习,整合信息技术、艺术或专业等方面的内容,以满足学生不同的个性、兴趣和职业发展需要。

2. 教学建议

中高职贯通教育英语教学应贯彻落实立德树人的指导思想,探索教与学的有效方式,以素养为指引,以目标为导向,以活动为载体,注重语言技能、语言知识和文化知识之间的融合以及各项语言技能之间的融合,培养学生的语言运用能力,逐步提升学生的学科核心素养。

语言技能、语言知识和文化知识的教学实施可以参考以下建议：

（1）语言技能

表 14　语言技能的教学建议

语言技能	教　学　建　议
视听技能	提供多样化的视听材料，注重教学方法与策略的使用，培养学生的视听技能。 1. 借助不同类型、题材的视听材料，例如影视片段、新闻广播等，激发学生的学习动机和兴趣； 2. 运用听前预测，提升学生信息筛选和推断能力； 3. 借助泛听与精听的综合训练，提升学生对语料主旨的推断与归纳能力，对细节信息的理解与推测能力，以及对语调、语气、肢体动作和图表等信息的感知和理解能力； 4. 结合联想、猜测、推断、记录等视听策略，提高学生对视听材料的理解程度和信息处理效率； 5. 利用多媒体设备、应用软件等，通过视听说结合、视听读结合和视听写结合等方式，实现视听技能教学的多样性。
口语技能	在生活和职场情境中进行口语教学活动，引导学生在语言实践中学习，提升语言交际能力。 1. 创设轻松的语言学习环境，帮助学生克服畏难心理，激励学生主动表达自己的观点和想法； 2. 利用数字技术，创设符合学生知识背景、认知能力和水平的生活与职场情境，培养学生主动使用英语进行交际的意识，例如：通过模拟求职面试，帮助学生学会面试问答的相关表达方式； 3. 引导学生借助语音、语调和节奏的变化，以及手势、表情等身势语提升沟通效果，体现情感态度，例如：根据场景的不同，采用正式或非正式、直接或婉转的表达方式，实现相应的交际功能； 4. 教学活动的组织应从封闭式向半封闭式、开放式过渡； 5. 指导学生运用重复、解释、转述、求助、延迟、提问等交际策略，克服交际障碍。
阅读技能	利用不同体裁和题材的阅读材料，设计凸显过程的阅读活动，帮助学生学会并运用阅读策略，提升语篇理解能力。 1. 促进合作阅读，例如：基于信息差开展阅读活动； 2. 引导学生借助题目、小标题和图表等信息，预测语篇主题和内容； 3. 引导学生运用略读策略把握文章大意和查读策略找出文中具体信息，提升文本理解能力； 4. 通过图片和实物展示、问题设置等方式，帮助学生在读前、读中、读后阶段建立阅读文本与生活、职业和周围世界的联系，激活与文本相关的背景知识，从而更好地理解文本； 5. 指导学生通过语篇研读，了解文章背景以及语篇所包含的语言知识和文化知识等，厘清文章结构与脉络，挖掘语篇的深层含义，加深对文本的理解。

续表

语言技能	教　学　建　议
写作技能	设计形式多样且符合学生认知能力的写作活动，逐步提高学生的写作能力。 1. 创设生活和职场情境，并提供足够的语言支撑，为学生完成写作任务搭建适用的脚手架； 2. 提供有指导的写作实践，例如：提供写作范文，引导学生从仿写入手，通过审题、构思、列提纲、起草、修改等环节，鼓励学生创建和完善写作文本，提高学生的书面表达能力； 3. 将写作与阅读、视听说教学有机结合，同时给予写作策略指导，例如：帮助学生分析阅读文本的写作框架、段落之间的衔接手段、句子之间的逻辑关系等，促进语言技能的融合，提升学生写作的规范性以及写作内容的一致性与连贯性。
翻译技能	帮助学生学习并掌握简单的英汉互译策略，并提供适量的翻译实践活动，使其具备基本的笔译和口译技能。 1. 在词汇、语法、视听、阅读等教学中渗透翻译教学，指导学生掌握英汉互译的基本方法，并在翻译实践中检测学生的学习效果； 2. 在确保源语意义不变的前提下，指导学生采用词性转换、词序调整等翻译技巧，例如：将英语中的副词、名词转换为汉语中的形容词，保证翻译的通顺与达意； 3. 在翻译句子时，引导学生解析句子结构，分析语态、时态等，提高词句表达的准确性； 4. 在翻译文本时，引导学生选用符合文本特征和语境的词汇，注意文本格式，确保翻译的规范性和适切性； 5. 在口译教学中，教师选择与生活或职场相关的视听素材，指导学生使用简单的英汉互译策略，例如：教会学生做简要记录，保证口译的准确度。

（2）语言知识

表 15　语言知识的教学建议

语言知识	教　学　建　议
语音知识	帮助学生形成语音意识，掌握发音规则和技巧，感受不同情境下语音的表意功能，克服语音导致的理解障碍。 1. 通过设计多样的语音实践活动，引导学生体验和感知不同语境下语音、语调的差异，了解发音规则和技巧，例如重音、节奏、连读、停顿、爆破等，从而有意识地进行语音知识的操练与运用； 2. 引导学生借助语音知识感知说话者的态度、意图和情感，同时表达自己的态度、意图和情感等； 3. 鼓励并组织学生参与不同形式的课内外活动，例如视频配音、诗歌朗诵、演讲比赛等，提升其语音、语调的准确性和表达的流畅度。

续 表

语言知识	教 学 建 议
词汇知识	指导学生在视听、口语、阅读、写作和翻译过程中感知与理解词汇的使用场景与固定搭配,积累词块,注重运用,强化语感,以达到词汇内化的目的。 1. 开展多样化的词汇学习活动,例如看图猜词、词汇配对、造句等,优化词汇教学,激发学生学习词汇的兴趣和动机; 2. 利用词族学习,帮助学生建立词汇间的联系,例如:运用思维导图进行词汇梳理和归类,扩大和巩固词汇量; 3. 引导学生借助词块学习,例如重要搭配和惯用语等,增强词汇意义的理解和记忆效果; 4. 引导学生基于构词法学习词汇,例如转化、派生和合成等,优化学生词汇理解和记忆效果; 5. 指导学生使用纸质和电子词典、词汇学习软件等工具,了解词汇的结构、意义和固定搭配等,以理解和掌握词汇的用法。
语法知识	组织学生在语境中学习语法,并与语言技能的教学有机结合,拓宽语法学习的渠道。 1. 在语境中教授语法,通过创设与生活和职场相关的情景,引导学生感知、理解语法的形式、意义与用法,并将语法运用于语言实践,例如:通过描述图片上人物的长相和着装特点,分析和提炼定语从句的基本结构; 2. 指导学生运用归纳法对语法规则进行梳理,例如:观察和比较图片中的人物信息,用比较级描述人物特征,从而归纳出比较级的不同用法; 3. 鼓励学生对比英汉语法结构的异同,找出规律,增强语法规则的理解与记忆效果; 4. 适当使用母语进行语法教学,优化教学效果; 5. 引导学生借助各类学习工具和资源,例如语法书、语法学习软件等,培养其自主解决语法问题的能力。
语篇知识	语篇教学既要讲授语篇知识,也要引导学生观察和分析语篇结构和语言特征,帮助学生强化语篇意识,掌握语篇知识,增进语篇理解,并选择适切语篇类型表达意义。 1. 帮助学生认识语音、词汇、语法等要素与语篇之间的关系,从而形成语篇意识,提升语篇理解能力; 2. 指导学生关注句与句、段与段、标题与正文、文字与图表之间的关系,以及句子和段落之间的衔接手段,例如:让学生找出连接词、过渡语等,以理解文本包含的结构与关系; 3. 引导学生通过不同类型语篇的学习,例如记叙文、说明文、议论文,尤其是职场常见的应用文,解析不同语篇的结构与特征,丰富学生的语篇知识; 4. 梳理语篇知识,帮助学生把握语篇的结构和语言特征,指导学生利用语篇知识进行有效的语言输出,达到运用语言表达思想、与人交流的目的。

续　表

语言知识	教　学　建　议
语用知识	语用知识的教学应聚焦语境和意义,帮助学生在特定语境中准确理解他人和得体表达自己的想法,最终达到有效交际的目的。 　　1. 通过播放视频、模拟场景对话、教师示范与讲解等方式,帮助学生感知语言的交际场合、交际参与者的身份与他们之间的关系; 　　2. 增强学生对交际场合、交际对象的情感距离或身份关系等的感知,引导学生采用直接或委婉、正式或非正式的表达方式,体现对交际对象应有的尊重和礼貌,确保交际得体有效; 　　3. 引导学生学习不同体裁的文本,例如记叙文、说明文、议论文,尤其是职场常见的应用文,掌握不同文体的语言表达方式和特征,并将语用知识正确运用到表达和交流之中; 　　4. 引导学生在与英语国家人士的交流过程中,基于其文化特点,尊重目标文化,避免文化禁忌,实现顺畅沟通。

(3) 文化知识

表 16　文化知识的教学建议

	教　学　建　议
文化知识	启发和引导学生学习中外优秀文化知识,通过对不同文化的感知、理解、比较、分析与取舍,将文化精髓内化为个人品格,并落实到行为之中。 　　1. 挖掘语篇中所包含的文化元素,帮助学生感知与理解文化知识; 　　2. 厘清语篇中所蕴含的文化背景,引导学生基于背景进行语言理解与表达; 　　3. 挖掘语篇的文化内涵,引导学生分析、讨论,加深对文化内涵与价值观的理解,并形成包容的态度; 　　4. 营造文化学习环境,开展形式多样的课内外活动,例如听英文歌曲、观看文化纪录片、介绍中国文化等,激发学生对文化学习的兴趣,丰富学生的文化学习生活,提升其民族文化自豪感,增强其文化自信。

（三）学习评价

评价是课程实施的重要组成部分和实现课程目标的重要保障。英语学科学习评价应基于学科核心素养,落实立德树人的根本任务;根据中高职贯通和五年一贯制人才培养的特点,制定一体化的学习评价方案,系统收集并科学分析学生学习表现的数据,全面考查学生的职场语言运用能力、跨文化理解能力和可持续学习能力;关注学生的学习过程,切实发挥评价的导向、激励、调节和改进作用。

1. 评价内容

围绕职场语言运用能力、跨文化理解能力和可持续学习能力等方面的要求,将文化自信、国际视野、合作意识、劳动精神等纳入评价范围,以一体化的方式确定评价内容。既关注学生对知识与技能的理解与掌握,又关注学生情感和态度的形成与发展;既关注学生学习的结果,更关注学生在学习过程中的感知、体验、实践与反思等。

2. 评价方式

坚持过程性评价与终结性评价相结合,积极探索并逐步实施增值性评价和表现性评价。根据不同的评价内容,采用纸笔测试、课堂观察、访谈、学生成长档案袋等不同评价方式;注重学生的语言实践表现,创设如角色扮演、演讲或辩论、制作海报等具有真实特征的评价任务,检测学生运用所学知识和技能完成真实性任务的能力。借助数字技术记录学生的学习过程和相关数据,以便更好地提供精准反馈和评估学生的学习;采用定性与定量相结合、主观与客观相结合等方法收集与分析数据,反馈与改进教学,促进课程目标的达成。

3. 评价主体

推进评价主体的多元化,除教育主管部门、学校和教师外,积极尝试引进行业企业专家和学生家长等社会力量参与评价;加强学生在评价中的主体地位,鼓励学生参与评价标准设计;倡导学生自评和互评,关注学生差异,指导学生通过自我反思和同伴评价调整和优化学习策略,提升职场语言运用能力、跨文化理解能力和可持续学习能力。

(四) 资源建设

中高职贯通教育英语课程资源是课程实施的重要组成部分,课程资源建设有助于拓宽教与学的渠道,增强教学资源的丰富性、开放性和灵活性,提升学生学习兴趣,推动学生核心素养的发展。在资源的整合与开发过程中应严格按照课程标准的要求，落实立德树人的根本任务，结合行业发展需求，为学生未来的职业发展和终身学习奠定基础。

1. 整合资源

教师应基于教与学的实际积极整合与利用各类中高职一体化课程资源。将校内外与学生生活息息相关的社团、图书馆、实践基地、网络空间、学习平台、家庭、社区、博物馆、科技馆、工厂等各种资源有机融入到英语课程资源中，并加以梳理与归类，建立立体化的课程资源库，引导学生开展校内校外、线上线下相融合的体验式学习。同时，教师应该根据所教学生的专业特点，加强与专业教师、行业和企业专家的合作，引入与学生未来工作行业相关的最新职业动态与要求，帮助学生了解行业与企业发展状况，熟悉企业文化，凸显英语教学的职教特色。

2. 开发资源

学校应吸纳一线骨干教师、英语课程与教学研究领域专家以及具有丰富经验的行业专家等社会力量，组成结构合理的资源开发团队，以确保开发资源的思想性、科学性、时代性以及趣味性。开发团队需根据本校学生的学习实际与需求，有计划、有组织地开发中高职一体化课程资源，例如教学平台、电子教案、课件以及其他数字化教学资源。同时需要加强调查研究和测试论证，广泛听取各方意见，重大问题向专家学者咨询，以求真务实、严谨细致的态度确保课程资源开发的质量，助力中高职贯通教育英语课程改革，促进学生学科核心素养的发展。

（五）保障措施

为了保障上海市中高职贯通教育英语课程标准的顺利实施，需要在管理制度、教师发展、保障条件三个方面采取切实措施。

1. 管理制度

各校需建立贯彻本课程标准的相关教学、评价和教研等管理制度，进行统筹安排与质量监控，确保落实各项管理规程，以制度建设推进中高职贯通教育，优化课程实施。

在相关部门指导下协调建立纵向联通、横向融合的教研组织架构，纵向联通市教研室、校际研修团队和校本教研团队,横向融合普通高校、普通高中以及各级教科研机构,并加强贯通院校之间的联合研修,形成教师专业学习共同体,实现合作互动、优势互补、资源共享,确保将本课程标准落到实处。

2. 教师发展

发挥本市中高职英语学科中心教研组织、名师工作室、学科带头人、骨干教师等的辐射、引领作用,通过各级各类理论与实践融合的英语研修活动,促进校际教研与同伴互助;重视教师梯队建设,打造具有示范引领作用的高端教师团队,扩展作为中坚力量的骨干教师团队,发展具有成长潜力的青年教师团队,为分层教研提供组织基础。

改革教学研究模式,推动教师聚焦教学实践中产生的普遍性与典型性问题,边实践、边研究,并将研究成果落实到课程实施之中,促进学生的有效学习,实现教师的专业发展。

3. 保障条件

学校应增加投入,加快具有职教特色的英语课程改革,大力改善英语教学环境,重视数字技术在教学中的地位与作用,加强线上线下课程资源的开发与利用,并推动行业企业参与教学实践,为中高职贯通教育英语课程实施提供有力的支持与保障。

附 录

附录1：交际功能项目表

1. 问候与道别（Greeting and saying goodbye）
2. 引荐与介绍（Introducing oneself and others）
3. 感谢与道歉（Expressing thanks and making apologies）
4. 预约与邀请（Making appointments and invitations）
5. 祝愿与祝贺（Expressing wishes and congratulations）
6. 意愿与打算（Expressing intentions and making plans）
7. 求助与提供帮助（Asking for and offering help）
8. 赞同与反对（Expressing agreement and disagreement）
9. 接受与拒绝（Accepting and rejecting）
10. 劝告与建议（Giving advice and making suggestions）
11. 判断与评论（Making judgments and comments）
12. 能够与不能够（Expressing possibility and impossibility）
13. 肯定与不肯定（Expressing certainty and uncertainty）
14. 满意与不满意（Expressing satisfaction and dissatisfaction）
15. 喜欢与不喜欢（Expressing likes and dislikes）
16. 遗憾与同情（Expressing regret and sympathy）
17. 询问与提供信息（Seeking and offering information）

18. 投诉与责备(Complaining and blaming)
19. 表扬与鼓励(Praising and encouraging)
20. 指令与要求(Giving instructions and making requests)
21. 禁止与警告(Prohibiting and warning)

附录2：话　　题

1. 个人信息（Personal information）
2. 日常生活（Daily life）
3. 休闲娱乐（Leisure and entertainment）
4. 健康饮食（Healthy diet）
5. 志愿服务（Volunteer work）
6. 科学技术（Science and technology）
7. 信息传媒（Information and media）
8. 工作就业（Jobs and employment）
9. 节日习俗（Festivals and customs）
10. 人类文明（Human civilization）
11. 多元文化（Multiculture）
12. 环境保护（Environmental protection）
13. 团队合作（Teamwork）
14. 职场礼仪（Workplace manners）
15. 职场安全（Workplace safety）
16. 职业发展（Career development）
17. 工匠精神（Craftsman spirit）
18. 创新创业（Innovation and entrepreneurship）

附录3：词 汇 表

本表共收录词汇 3129 个，包括基础模块词汇 2624 个和拓展模块一（基础拓展）词汇 505 个（用 * 标记）。

	A		
	a/an	*	accompany
*	abandon	*	accomplish
	ability		according
	able		account
*	abnormal		accountant
	aboard	*	accurate
	about		accuse
	above		ache
	abroad		achieve
	absent	*	acid
	absolute	*	acknowledge
*	absorb		acquire
*	abstract		across
*	abuse		act
*	academic		active
	accent		activity
	accept		actor/actress
	access		actual
	accident	*	AD
*	accommodation		adapt
			add

	addict		again
	address		against
	adjust		age
*	administration		agency
	admire	*	agenda
	admit		agent
*	adopt		ago
*	adorable		agree
	adult		agriculture
	advance		ahead
	advanced		AI/artificial intelligence
	advantage		aid
	adventure		aim
	advertise/advertize		air
	advertisement/advertizement/ad		airline
	advice		airport
	advise		aisle
*	advocate		alarm
	aeroplane/plane		album
	affair		alcohol
	affect		alert
	afford		alike
	afraid		alive
	after		all
	afternoon		allow
	afterwards		almost

	alone		anger
	along	*	angle
*	alongside		angry
	aloud		animal
	already	*	ankle
	alright		announce
	also		annoy
	alter		annual
*	alternative		another
	although		answer
	altogether		ant
	always	*	anticipate
	am/a.m./AM/A.M.	*	antique
*	amateur		anxious
	amaze		any
*	ambition		anybody/anyone
	ambulance		anyhow
*	amendment		anymore
	among		anything
	amount		anyway
	amuse		anywhere
*	analyse/analyze		apart
*	ancestor		apartment
	ancient		apologise/apologize
	and		apparent
	angel		appeal

续 表

	appear			as
	appetite			ashamed
*	applaud			aside
	apple			ask
	apply			asleep
	appoint			aspect
	appreciate		*	assess
	approach		*	asset
*	appropriate		*	assign
*	approve			assist
*	AR/augmented reality			assistant
*	arch			associate
*	architect			assume
	area		*	assumption
	argue			assure
*	arise		*	astonish
	arm		*	astronaut
	army		*	astronomer
	around			at
	arrange			athlete
	arrest			ATM/automated teller machine
	arrive			atmosphere
*	arrow			attach
	art			attack
	article		*	attain
*	artificial			attempt

	attend		background
	attention		backward
	attitude		bacon
	attract		bad
	audience		badminton
	aunt		bag
	author		bake
	authority		bakery
	automatic		balance
	automobile/auto		ball
*	autonomous		ballet
	autumn/fall		balloon
	available		bamboo
*	avenue	*	ban
	average		banana
	avoid		band
	awake		bang
	award		bank
	aware		bar
	away		barbecue
	awesome		bare
	awful		bark
	awkward	*	barrier
	B		base
	baby		basic
	back		basin

续 表

	basis			behaviour/behavior
	basket			behind
	bat		*	being
	bath		*	belief
	battery			believe
	battle			bell
	bay			belong
*	BC			below
	be			belt
	beach			bend
	bean			beneath
	bear			benefit
	beard			beside
	beat			besides
	beauty			best
	because			bet
	become			better
	bed			between
	bee			beyond
	beef			bicycle/bike
	beer			big
	before			bill
	beg			billion
	begin			bin
*	behalf			bind
*	behave			biology

续 表

	bird		bond
	birth		bone
	biscuit	*	bonus
	bit		book
	bite		booklet
	bitter		boom
	black	*	boost
	blame		boot
	blank		border
	blanket	*	bore
	bleed		boring
	bless		born
	blind		borrow
	block		boss
	blog	*	botanical
	blonde		both
	blood		bother
	bloom		bottle
	blouse		bottom
	blow		bounce
	blue	*	boundary
	board		bow
	boat		bowl
	body	*	bowling
	boil		box
	bomb		boxing

	boy		buck
	brain		bucket
	brake		budget
	branch	*	buffet
	brand		bug
	brave		build
	bread		bump
	break		bunch
	breakfast		burger
	breast		burn
	breath		burst
	breathe		bury
	breed		bus
	brick		bush
	bride/bridegroom		business
	bridge		busy
	brief		but
	bright	*	butcher
	brilliant		butter
	bring		button
	broad		buy
	broadcast		by
	brochure		bye/goodbye
	brother		**C**
	brown	*	cabbage
	brush		cabin

续 表

	cable	*	capacity
	cafe/café		cape
*	cafeteria		capital
	cage	*	capsule
	cake		captain
	calculate	*	capture
	calendar		car
	call		carbon
*	calligraphy		card
	calm		care
*	calorie		career
*	camel		cargo
	camera		carpet
	camp		carrot
*	campaign		carry
	campus		cart
	can		cartoon
*	canal	*	carve
	cancel		case
	cancer		cash
*	candidate		cashier
	candle		cast
	candy		castle
*	canteen		casual
	cap		cat
	capable		catch

*	category		channel
	cattle	*	chaos
	cause		chapter
	caution		character
*	cave		charge
*	cease		charity
	ceiling		charm
	celebrate	*	chart
*	celebrity		chase
	cell		chat
	cent		cheap
	centimetre/centimeter		cheat
	centre/center		check
	century		cheek
	cereal		cheer
	certain		cheese
	certificate		chef
	chain		chemical
	chair		chemistry
	chairman/chairwoman/chairperson		cheque/check
	chalk		chess
	challenge		chest
*	champagne		chew
	champion		chicken
	chance		chief
	change		child

续 表

	childhood		clarify
	chilli/chili		class
	chip		classic
	chocolate		classical
	choice	*	clay
*	choke		clean
	choose		clear
	chop		clerk
	chopsticks		clever
	chore		click
*	chorus	*	client
	Christmas		cliff
	church		climate
	cigarette		climb
	cinema		clinic
	circle		clip
*	circuit		clock
	circumstance	*	clone
*	circus	*	cloning
*	cite		close
	citizen		cloth
	city		clothes
*	civil		cloud
*	civilian		clown
	claim		club
	clap		clue

续 表

	coach		commit
	coal		committee
	coast		common
	coat		communicate
	code	*	communist
	coffee		community
	coin		company
	cold		compare
*	collapse		compete
*	collar	*	competence
	colleague		competition
	collect		complain
	college	*	complaint
	colour/color		complete
*	column	*	complex
	comb		complicate
	combine	*	component
	come	*	compose
*	comedy	*	comprehensive
	comfort	*	comprise
	comic		computer
	command		concentrate
	comment	*	concept
	commerce		concern
	commercial		concert
*	commission	*	conclude

续表

*	concrete		content
	condition	*	contest
	conduct		context
	conference		continent
	confidence		continue
	confident		contract
	confirm	*	contradictory
	conflict	*	contrary
*	Confucius	*	contrast
	confuse		contribute
	congratulation		control
	connect		convenient
	conscious	*	conventional
*	consequence		conversation
*	conservative		convince
	consider		cook
*	consist		cookie
	consistent		cool
	constant		cooperate
*	constitution		cop
	construct		cope
*	consult		copy
*	consume	*	core
	contact		corn
	contain		corner
*	contemporary	*	corporation

	correct			crazy
*	correspond			cream
	cost			create
*	costume			creative
	cottage			creature
	cotton			credit
	cough			creep
	could		*	crew
	council			crime
	count			criminal
	counter		*	crisis
	country			crisp
	county		*	criterion
	couple		*	critical
*	coupon			criticise/criticize
	courage		*	crop
	course			cross
	court			crowd
	cousin			crown
	cover		*	crucial
	cow			cruel
	crack			cry
	craft		*	cuisine
	crash			culture
	crawl			cup
	crayon			cupboard

	cure		dawn
	curious		day
	curl		dead
	current		deadline
	curry		deaf
	curtain		deal
	custom		dear
	customer		death
	cut	*	debate
	cute		debt
	cycle	*	decade
	D		decent
	dad		decide
	daily		decision
	dairy		deck
	damage		declare
*	damp	*	decline
	dance		decorate
	danger	*	decrease
	dare	*	dedicate
	dark		deep
	darling		deer
	data	*	defeat
	database		defence/defense
	date	*	defend
	daughter	*	deficit

续　表

	definite			desperate
*	definition			despite
	degree			dessert
	delay			destination
*	delete			destroy
*	delicate			detail
	delicious			detect
	delight			determine
	deliver			develop
	demand			device
*	democratic		*	devote
*	demonstrate			diagram
	dentist			dialogue/dialog
	deny		*	diamond
	department			diary
	departure		*	dictation
	depend			dictionary
	deposit			die
	depress			diet
*	depth		*	differ
	describe			difference
	desert			different
	deserve			difficult
	design			dig
	desire		*	digest
	desk			digital

续 表

*	dignity		*	distinct
*	dimension		*	distinguish
	dine		*	distribution
	dinner			district
*	dinosaur			disturb
	diploma			dive
	direct		*	diverse
	directed			divide
*	directory			divorce
	dirty		*	dizzy
	disabled			do
	disappear			doctor/Dr.
	disappoint			document
	disaster			dog
	discipline			doll
	discount			dollar
	discover			dolphin
*	discrimination		*	domain
	discuss		*	domestic
	disease		*	dominate
	disgust			donate
	dish			door
*	disk			dormitory/dorm
*	dismiss			double
	display			doubt
	distance			down

	download		dust
	downtown		duty
	dozen	*	dynamic
	draft		dynasty
	drag		**E**
	dragon		each
	drama		eager
	draw	*	eagle
	drawer		ear
	dream		early
	dress		earn
*	drill		earth
	drink		earthquake
	drive		ease
	drop		east
	drought		easy
	drug		eat
	drum	*	ecology
	dry		economic
	duck		economy
	due	*	e-currency
	dull		edge
	dump		edit
	dumpling		educate
*	duration		effect
	during		effective

续 表

	efficient			enable
	effort		*	encounter
	egg			encourage
	either			end
	elder			enemy
	elect			energy
	electric			engage
	electricity			engine
	electronic			engineer
*	elegant		*	enhance
	element			enjoy
	elephant			enormous
*	eliminate			enough
	else			ensure
*	elsewhere			enter
	email/e-mail		*	enterprise
	embarrass			entertain
*	embrace		*	enthusiastic
*	emerge			entire
	emergency		*	entitle
	emotion			entrance
*	emperor			entry
*	emphasis			envelope
	empire			environment
	employ		*	envy
	empty		*	episode

续 表

	equal		evidence
	equipment		evil
*	era		exact
	eraser		examination/exam
	error		examine
*	erupt		example
	escape		excellent
	especially		except
*	essay	*	exceptional
	essential		exchange
	establish		excite
	estate		excuse
*	estimate	*	executive
	euro		exercise
*	evaluate		exhaust
	eve		exhibition
	even		exist
	evening		exit
	event	*	expand
	eventually		expect
	ever		expense
	every		expensive
	everyday		experience
	everyone/everybody		experiment
	everything		expert
	everywhere		explain

续 表

*	explode		fall
	explore		false
	export		familiar
	expose		family
	express		famous
	extend		fan
	extent		fancy
	external		fantastic
	extinction		far
	extra		fare
*	extraordinary		farm
	extreme		fascinate
	eye		fashion
	F		fast
*	fabric		fat
	face		father
	facility		fault
	fact		favour/favor
	factor		favourite/favorite
	factory		fax
	fail		fear
	failure		feather
	faint		feature
	fair	*	federal
	fairy		fee
	faith		feed

续　表

	feel		firm
	fellow		fish
	female	*	fist
	fence		fit
	festival		fix
	fetch		flag
	fever		flame
	few		flash
*	fiber		flat
*	fiction		flavour/flavor
	field		flexible
	fight		flight
	figure		flip
	file		float
	fill		flood
	film		floor
	final	*	flour
	finance		flow
	find		flower
	fine		flu
	finger		fluent
	finish		fly
	fire		focus
	firefighter		fog
	fireplace		fold
	firework		folk

续 表

	follow	*	foundation
	fond	*	fountain
	food		fox
	fool	*	fragile
	foot		frame
	football		frankly
	for		free
	force		freeze
	forecast		frequent
	forehead		fresh
	foreign	*	friction
	forest		friend
	forever		friendly
	forget		fright
	forgive		frog
	fork		from
	form		front
	formal	*	frontier
*	format		frost
	former		fruit
	fortnight		frustrate
	fortunate		fry
	fortune		fuel
	forum		full
	forward		fun
*	found		function

	fund			generous
*	fundamental		*	genius
	fur			gentle
	furniture			gentleman
	further		*	genuine
	future			geography
	G		*	geometry
	gain			gesture
*	gallery			get
*	gallon			ghost
	game			giant
	gap			gift
	garage			giraffe
*	garbage			girl
	garden			give
	garlic			glad
	gas			glance
	gate			glass
	gather			global
*	gay			glory
	gear			glove
	gender			glue
*	gene			go
	general			goal
*	generate		*	goat
	generation			god

续 表

	gold		greedy
	golf		green
	good		greenhouse
	goods		greet
	gorgeous		grey/gray
	govern		grilled
	government		grin
	grab		grocer
	grace		ground
	grade		group
*	gradually		grow
	graduate		guarantee
*	grain		guard
	grammar		guess
	gramme/gram		guest
	grand		guide
	grandchild/grandson/granddaughter		guideline
	grandparent/grandfather/granddad/grandpa/grandmother/grandma		guilty
			guitar
	grant		gun
	grape		guy
	grasp		gymnasium/gym
	grass		gymnastics
	grateful		**H**
*	gravity		habit
	great	*	habitat

续　表

	hair		head
	hairdresser		headline
	half		headmaster
	hall		health
	ham		heap
	hammer		hear
	hand		heart
*	handkerchief		heat
	handle		heaven
	handsome		heavy
*	handwriting		hedge
	handy		height
	hang		hell
	happen		hello
	happy		help
	hard		hen
	hardly	*	hence
	hardware		her
	harm	*	herb
*	harmony		here
	harvest		hero
	hat		hers
*	hatch		herself
	hate		hesitate
	have		hide
	he		high

*	highlight		hope
	high-tech		horrible
	highway		horse
	hike		hospital
	hill		host
	him		hostess
	himself		hot
	hip-hop		hotel
	hire		hour
	his		house
	historical		household
	history		housewife
	hit		housework
	hobby		how
*	hockey		however
	hold		hug
	hole		huge
	holiday		human
	home	*	humble
	homeland		humour/humor
	hometown		hundred
	homework		hunger
	honest		hunt
	honey	*	hurricane
	honor		hurry
	hook		hurt

	husband		in
*	hydrogen		inch
	I	*	incident
	I		include
	ice		income
	idea		increase
*	ideal		incredible
	identify		indeed
	identity		independent
*	idiom		indicate
	idiot		individual
	if		industry
	ignore	*	infect
	ill	*	infer
	illustrate		influence
	image		inform
	imagine		informal
	immediate	*	infrastructure
*	immigrant	*	initial
	impact	*	initiative
*	implement		injure
*	imply		inn
	import	*	inner
	important		innocent
	impress	*	innovation
	improve		input

续表

*	inquire		Internet/Net
	insect	*	internship
*	insert	*	interpret
	inside		interrupt
*	insight	*	intervention
	insist		interview
	inspect		into
	inspire		introduce
	install		invent
	instance		invest
	instant		investigate
	instead		invite
	institute	*	invoice
	instruct		involve
	instrument		IOT/Internet of things
	insure		iron
*	integrate		island
*	integrity		issue
	intelligent		it
	intend		IT/information technology
	intense		item
	intent		its
*	interaction		itself
	interest		**J**
*	internal		jacket
	international		jam

续 表

	jaw		*	kettle
	jazz			key
	jeans			keyboard
	jewellery/jewelry			kick
	job			kid
	jog			kill
	join			kilogramme/kilogram/kilo
*	joint			kilometre/kilometer
	joke			kind
	journal			kindergarten
*	journalist			king
	journey		*	kingdom
	joy			kiss
	judge			kit
	juice			kitchen
	jump			kite
*	jungle			knee
	junior			knife
*	jury			knit
	just			knock
	justice			know
*	justify			knowledge
	K			**L**
	kangaroo			label
	keen			laboratory/lab
	keep			labour/labor

续 表

	lack		lay
	ladder	*	layer
	lady		lazy
	lake		lead
	lamb		leaf
	lamp		league
	land	*	leak
*	landscape		lean
	lane		leap
	language		learn
	lantern		least
	lap		leather
	laptop/lap-top		leave
	large		lecture
	laser		left
	last		leg
	late		legal
	later		leisure
	latest		lemon
	latter		lemonade
	laugh		lend
*	launch		length
	laundry		less
	law		lesson
	lawn		let
	lawyer		letter

续　表

	level			little
*	liberal			live
*	liberty			load
	library			loaf
	licence/license			loan
	lid			lobby
	lie			local
	life			locate
	lift			lock
	light		*	lockdown
	lightly			log
	lightning		*	logical
	like			lone
	likely			lonely
	limit			long
	line			look
	link			loose
	lion			lord
	lip			lose
	liquid			loss
	list			lost
	listen			lot
*	literally			loud
*	literary			love
	litre/liter			lovely
	litter			low

续 表

	lower		manner
	luck		manufacture
	luggage		many
	lump		map
	lunar	*	marathon
	lunch		march
*	lung		mark
	luxury		market
	M		marry
	machine		marvel
	mad		mask
	madam		mass
	magazine	*	massage
	magic		massive
	mail		master
	main		match
	mainland		mate
	maintain		material
	major		mathematics/maths/math
	make		matter
	make-up	*	mature
	male		maximum/max
	man		may
	manage		maybe
	mango		mayor
*	mankind		me

续 表

	meal		metal
	mean		method
	means		metre/meter
*	meanwhile	*	microscope
	measure		microwave
	meat		middle
	mechanic		midnight
	medal		might
	medical		mild
	medicine		mile
	medium		military
	meet		milk
	melon		mill
	melt	*	millimetre/millimeter
	member		million
	memo		mind
*	memorial		mine
	memory	*	mineral
	mental	*	minimum
	mention		minister
	menu		minor
*	mercy		minus
*	merely		minute
	merry		miracle
	mess		mirror
	message		miss

续 表

*	missile		*	motivate
	mission		*	motive
*	mist			motor
	mistake			motorway
	mix		*	motto
	mobile			mount
*	mode			mountain
	model			mouse
	modern			mouth
	moment			move
	money			movie
	monitor			mow
	monkey			Mr/Mr.
	month			Mrs/Mrs.
	mood			Ms/Ms.
	moon			much
*	mop			mud
*	moral			mug
	more		*	multiple
	moreover			mum
	morning			murder
	mosque			muscle
*	mosquito			museum
	most		*	mushroom
	mother			music
*	motion			musician

续　表

	must		negative
*	mutton	*	negotiate
	my		neighbour/neighbor
	myself		neighbourhood/neighborhood
	mystery		neither
	N		nephew
	nail		nerve
	name		nervous
	nanny		nest
	narrow	*	net
	nasty		network
	nation		never
	nationality	*	nevertheless
	native		new
	nature		news
	naughty		newspaper
	navy		next
	near		nice
	nearby		niece
	nearly		night
	neat		no
	necessary	*	noble
	neck		nobody
	necklace		nod
	need		noise
	needle		non

	none		objective
	noodle		observe
	noon	*	obtain
	nor		obvious
	normal		occasion
	north		occupation
	northern	*	occupy
	nose		occur
	not		ocean
	note		o'clock
	nothing		odd
	notice		of
*	notion		off
	novel	*	offense
	now		offer
	nowadays		office
	nowhere		officer
*	nuclear		official
	number		often
*	numerous		oil
	nurse		okay/OK
	nut		old
*	nutrition		Olympic
	O		omelette/omelet
	obey		on
	object		once

	oneself		other
	onion		otherwise
	online/on-line		ought
	only		our
	onto		ours
	open		ourselves
	opera		out
	operate	*	outcome
	opinion		outgoing
*	opponent	*	outline
	opportunity		output
	oppose		outstanding
	opposite		oven
*	optimistic		over
	option	*	overall
	or	*	overcome
*	oral		overseas
	orange		owe
*	orbit		own
	order		owned
	ordinary		oxygen
*	organ	**P**	
*	organic	*	pace
	organise/organize		pack
*	origin		package
	original		page

续 表

	pain		*	passion
	paint			passive
	pair			passport
	pal			password
	palace			past
	pale			pasta
	pan			pat
	pancake			patch
	panda		*	patent
*	pandemic			path
*	panel			patient
	panic			pattern
	paper			pause
	paragraph			pay
	parcel			PC/personal computer
	pardon			PE/physical education
	parent			pea
	park			peace
	part		*	peak
	participate			pear
	particular			pen
	partner			pencil
	party			penny
	pass			pension
	passage			people
	passenger			pepper

续　表

	per		physics
*	perceive		piano
	percent		pick
*	perception		picnic
	perfect		picture
	perform		pie
	perhaps		piece
	period		pig
*	permanent		pile
	permit		pill
	person		pillow
*	personnel		pilot
*	perspective		pin
	persuade		pine
*	pessimistic		pink
	pet		pioneer
	petrol		pipe
*	phase		pitch
*	phenomenon		pity
*	philosophy		pizza
	photograph/photo		place
	photographer		plain
	photography		plan
*	phrase		planet
	physical		plant
*	physician		plastic

续 表

		plate			pollute
		platform	*		pond
		play			pool
		pleasant			poor
		please			pop
		pleasure			popular/pop
		plenty			population
*		plot			pork
		plug			port
		plumber	*		portion
		plural	*		pose
		plus			position
		pm/p.m./PM/P.M.			positive
		pocket			possess
		poem			possible
		poet			post
		point			poster
		poison			postpone
*		polar			pot
		pole			potato
		police	*		potential
		policy			pound
		polish			pour
		polite	*		poverty
		politics			powder
*		poll			power

续　表

	practical		primary
	practice		prime
	practise/practice	*	primitive
	praise		prince
	pray	*	principle
	precaution		print
*	precious	*	prior
*	precisely		prison
*	predict		privacy
	prefer		private
	pregnant		prize
*	prejudice		probably
*	premier		problem
	prepare		procedure
	present	*	proceed
*	preserve		process
	president		produce
	press		product
	pressure		profession
	presume		professor
	pretend		profile
	pretty		profit
	prevent		programme/program
	previous		progress
	price	*	prohibit
	pride		project

续表

	promise		pup
	promote		pupil
	pronounce		purchase
*	proof		pure
	proper		purple
	property		purpose
	proposal	*	purse
	propose	*	pursue
*	prospect		push
	protect		put
*	protein		puzzle
	protest		**Q**
	proud		qualify
	prove		quality
	provide		quantity
	province	*	quarantine
*	psychology		quarter
	pub		queen
	public		question
	publish		queue
	pudding		quick
	pull		quiet
	pump		quit
	pumpkin		quite
	punch		quiz
	punish		quote

	R		real
	rabbit		realise/realize
	race	*	realistic
	racket		reason
*	radiation		recall
	radio		receipt
*	radium		receive
	railway		recent
	rain		reception
*	rainbow		receptionist
	raise		recipe
*	random	*	recite
	range		reckon
*	rank		recognise/recognize
	rap		recognition
	rapid		recommend
	rare		record
	rat		recover
	rate	*	recreation
	rather		recycle
	raw		red
	ray		reduce
	reach		refer
	react		reflect
	read	*	reform
	ready	*	refresh

续 表

	refrigerator/fridge		rent
	refund		repair
	refuse		repeat
	regard		replace
	region		reply
	register		report
	regret		represent
	regular		representative
*	regulation		republic
	reject	*	reputation
	relate		request
	relative		require
	relax	*	rescue
*	relay		research
	release		reserve
*	relevant		resident
	relief	*	resign
*	religious		resist
	rely	*	resistance
	remain	*	resolve
	remark		resort
*	remarkable		resource
	remember		respect
	remind	*	respective
*	remote		respond
	remove		responsible

续 表

	rest		*	ripe
	restaurant			rise
*	restore			risk
*	restrict			river
	result			road
	resume			roar
	retire			roast
	return			rob
	reveal			robot
*	revenue			rock
	review			rocket
	revise			role
*	revolution			roll
	reward			romantic
*	rhyme			roof
	rice			room
	rich			root
	rid			rope
*	riddle			rose
	ride			rot
	ridiculous			rough
	rift			round
	right			roundabout
*	rigid			route
	ring		*	routine
	rip			row

	royal		satisfy
	rub		sauce
	rubbish	*	saucer
	rude		sausage
	rugby		save
	ruin		say
	rule	*	saying
	run		scale
*	rural		scan
	rush		scare
	S		scarf
	sad		scene
	safe		scenery
	safety		schedule
	sail	*	scholarship
	saint		school
	sake		science
	salad		scientific
	salary		scissors
	sale		score
	salt		scratch
	same		scream
	sample		screen
	sand		screw
	sandwich	*	sculpture
*	satellite		sea

续　表

	seal		separate
	search		series
	season		serious
	seat	*	servant
	second		serve
*	secondary		service
	seconds	*	session
	secret		set
	secretary	*	setting
	section		settle
*	sector		several
	secure	*	severe
	see		sew
	seed		sex
	seek		shade
	seem		shadow
	seize		shake
	seldom		shall
	select		shallow
	self		shame
	sell		shampoo
	send		shape
	senior		share
	sense	*	shark
*	sensitive		sharp
	sentence		shave

续 表

	she		sick
	shed		side
	sheep		sight
	sheet		sign
	shelf		signal
	shell	*	signature
	shelter		significant
	shift		silence
	shine		silent
	ship		silk
	shirt		silly
	shiver		silver
	shock		similar
	shoe		simple
	shoot		since
	shop		sincere
	shore		sing
	short		single
	should		singular
	shoulder		sink
	shout		sir
	shove		sister
	show		sit
	shower		site
	shut		situation
	shy		size

续　表

	skate		snap
	ski		sneaker
	skill	*	sneeze
	skin		snow
	skip		so
	skirt		soap
	sky		soccer
	slave		social
	sleep	*	socialist
*	sleeve		society
	slice		sock
	slide		sofa
	slight		soft
	slim		software
	slip		soil
	slow	*	solar
	small		soldier
	smart		solid
	smash		solution
	smell		solve
	smile		some
	smog		somebody
	smoke		somehow
	smooth		someone
	snack		something
	snake		sometimes

续 表

	somewhat			speech
	somewhere			speed
	son			spell
	song			spend
	soon			spin
	sore			spirit
*	sorrow			spit
	sorry		*	splendid
	sort			split
	soul			spoil
	sound		*	sponsor
	soup			spoon
	sour			sport
	source			spot
	south			spray
	southern			spread
*	souvenir			spring
*	sow		*	spy
	space			square
	spaceship		*	stability
	spare			stable
	speak			stadium
	special			staff
	specialty			stage
	species			stair
	specific			stamp

	stand			stomach
	standard			stone
	star			stop
	stare			storage
	start			store
	starve			storey/story
	state			storm
	station			story
*	stationery			straight
*	statistic		*	strait
*	statue			strange
*	status			strategy
	stay			strawberry
	steady			stream
	steak			street
	steal			strength
	steam			stress
	steel			stretch
	step			strict
*	steward			strike
	stick			string
	stiff			strip
	still			stroke
*	stimulate			strong
	stir		*	structure
	stock			struggle

续 表

	student			sum
	studio			summary
	study			summer
	stuff			sun
	stupid			super
	style		*	superb
	subject		*	superior
*	subjective			supper
*	submit			supply
*	subscribe			support
*	subsequent			suppose
*	substance			sure
	suburb			surf
	subway			surface
	succeed		*	surgery
	success			surname
	such			surprise
	suck			surround
	sudden			surroundings
	suffer			survey
	sufficient			survive
	sugar			suspect
	suggest		*	suspend
	suit			suspicion
	suitcase		*	sustain
	suite			swallow

续 表

	swear		tame
	sweat		tank
	sweater		tap
	sweep		tape
	sweet		target
	swim		task
	swing		taste
	switch		tax
	sword		taxi
	symbol		tea
	sympathy		teach
*	symphony		team
	symptom		tear
	system		tease
	T		technical
	table		technician
*	tablet		technique
*	tackle		technology
	tag		teenage
	tail		telephone/phone
*	tailor	*	telescope
	take		television/TV
	tale		tell
	talent		temperature
	talk		temple
	tall	*	temporary

续　表

	tempt			therefore
	tend			these
*	tender			they
	tennis			thick
	tense			thief
	tent			thin
	term			thing
*	terminal			think
	terrible			thirst
*	territory			this
	test		*	thorough
	text			those
	than			though
	thank			thought
	that			thousand
	the			thread
	theatre/theater			threat
*	theft			throat
	their			through
	them			throughout
	theme			throw
	themselves			thunder
	then			thus
*	theory			tick
*	therapy			ticket
	there			tide

续 表

	tidy		tone
	tie		tongue
	tiger		tonight
	tight		too
	till		tool
	time		tooth
	timetable		top
	timid		topic
	tin	*	torch
	tiny		total
	tip		touch
	tire		tough
	tissue		tour
	title	*	tournament
	to		toward
	toast		towel
*	tobacco		tower
	today		town
	toe		toy
	tofu		trace
	together		track
	toilet		trade
*	tolerate		tradition
	tomato		traffic
	tomorrow	*	trail
	ton		train

续 表

	transfer			*	tunnel
*	transform				turkey
*	transition				turn
	translate			*	tutor
	transport				twice
	trap				twin
	travel				twist
	tray				type
	treasure				typhoon
	treat				typical
	tree				tyre/tire
	trend				**U**
	trial				ugly
	trick			*	ultimately
	trip				umbrella
*	troop				uncle
	trouble				under
	trousers				underground
	truck				underline
	true				underneath
	trunk				understand
	trust				unforgettable
	truth				unfortunately
	try				uniform
*	tube				union
	tune				unique

	unit	*	variable
	unite		variety
	universe		various
*	universe		vary
	university	*	vase
	unknown		vast
	unless		vegetable
	unlike		vehicle
	until/till	*	venue
	up		version
	update		very
	upon	*	vet
	upper	*	veteran
	upset	*	via
	urban	*	vice
*	urge		victim
	urgent		victory
	us		video
	use		view
	used		village
	usual	*	violence
	V		violent
	vacation		violin
	valley		virtual
	value	*	virtue
	van		virus

续 表

	visa			wallet
*	visible			wander
*	vision			want
	visit			war
*	visual		*	ward
*	vital			warm
	vitamin			warn
*	vivid			wash
	vocabulary			waste
	vocation			watch
	voice			water
	volcano			watermelon
	volleyball		*	waterproof
	volume			wave
	volunteer			way
	vote			we
*	voyage			weak
*	VR/virtual reality			wealth
	W			weapon
	wage			wear
*	waist			weather
	wait			web
	waiter/waitress			wed
	wake			weed
	walk			week
	wall			weekly

*	weep		whole
	weigh		whom
	weight		whose
	weird		why
	welcome		wicked
*	welfare		wide
	well		width
	well-known		wife
	west		Wi-Fi
	western		wild
	wet		will
	whale		win
	what		wind
	wheat		window
	wheel		wine
	when		wing
	where		winter
	whereas		wipe
	whether		wire
	which		wisdom
	while		wise
	whip		wish
*	whisper		with
	whistle	*	withdraw
	white		within
	who		without

续　表

	witness		**X**
	wolf		X-ray
	woman		**Y**
	wonder		yard
	wood		yeah/yeh
	wool		year
	word		yell
	work		yellow
	workshop		yes
	world		yesterday
	worm		yet
	worry		yogurt/yoghurt
	worse		you
	worth		young
*	worthwhile		your
	would		yours
	wound		yourself
	wrap		youth
*	wrestle		**Z**
*	wrinkle		zero
*	wrist		zone
	write		zoo
	wrong	*	zoom

附录 4：中华优秀传统文化常用词汇

1. Ancient Thoughts 古代思想

Confucianism 儒家思想

Taoism/Daoism 道家思想；道教

Legalism 法家思想

Buddhism 佛教

yin and yang 阴阳

five elements (metal, wood, water, fire and earth)/wuxing 五行(金、木、水、火、土)

eight trigrams 八卦

heavenly stems 天干

earthly branches 地支

Oneness of Heaven and Human 天人合一

Unity of Knowledge and Action 知行合一

2. Festivals and Customs 节日习俗

the Spring Festival 春节

Chinese New Year's Eve 除夕

the Lantern Festival 元宵节

Tomb-Sweeping Day/Qingming Festival 清明节

the Dragon Boat Festival 端午节

the Double Seventh Festival/the Qixi Festival/the Magpie Festival 七夕

the Mid-Autumn Festival 中秋节

the Double Ninth Festival 重阳节

lunar calendar 农历

the Spring Festival Gala 春晚

Spring Festival reunion dinner/Chinese New Year reunion dinner 年夜饭

red packet/red envelope 红包

lucky money 压岁钱

firework 烟花,烟火

firecracker 鞭炮

couplet 对联

New Year painting 年画

paper-cut 剪纸

door god 门神

temple fair 庙会

lantern 灯笼,花灯

lantern riddle 灯谜

dragon dance 舞龙

lion dance 舞狮

the God of Wealth 财神

spring outing 踏青

dragon boat 龙舟

perfume pouch 香包

3. The Twenty-four Solar Terms 二十四节气

Beginning of Spring 立春

Rain Water 雨水

Awakening of Insects 惊蛰

Spring Equinox 春分

Pure Brightness 清明

Grain Rain 谷雨

Beginning of Summer 立夏

Grain Buds 小满

Grain in Ear 芒种

Summer Solstice 夏至

Minor Heat 小暑

Major Heat 大暑

Beginning of Autumn 立秋

Limit of Heat 处暑

White Dew 白露

Autumn Equinox 秋分

Cold Dew 寒露

Frost's Descent 霜降

Beginning of Winter 立冬

Minor Snow 小雪

Major Snow 大雪

Winter Solstice 冬至

Minor Cold 小寒

Major Cold 大寒

4. The Chinese Zodiac 生肖

Rat（生肖）子鼠

Ox（生肖）丑牛

Tiger（生肖）寅虎

Rabbit（生肖）卯兔

Dragon（生肖）辰龙

Snake（生肖）巳蛇

Horse（生肖）午马

Goat（生肖）未羊

Monkey（生肖）申猴

Rooster（生肖）酉鸡

Dog（生肖）戌狗

Pig（生肖）亥猪

5. Traditional Food 传统饮食

dumpling 饺子

rice dumpling/zongzi 粽子

sweet green rice ball 青团

spring roll 春卷

steamed twisted roll 花卷

rice cake 年糕

glutinous rice ball/tangyuan 汤圆,元宵

wonton 馄饨

stinky tofu 臭豆腐

hairy crab 大闸蟹

Beijing Roast Duck 北京烤鸭

Dongpo pork 东坡肉

hot pot 火锅

soybean milk 豆浆

Chinese rice wine 米酒

6. Places of Interest and Architecture 名胜古迹与建筑

the Great Wall 长城

the Forbidden City 故宫（紫禁城）

the Palace Museum 故宫博物院

the Summer Palace 颐和园

the Temple of Heaven 天坛

Yu Garden 豫园

the Bund 外滩

Guangfulin Cultural Relics Site 广富林文化遗址

the Terra-Cotta Warriors and Horses 兵马俑

Mogao Grottoes/Caves 敦煌莫高窟

the Sun Yat-sen Mausoleum 中山陵

Confucian temple 孔庙

the Temple of Town God 城隍庙

pagoda 佛塔

pavilion 亭,阁

bell tower 钟楼

drum tower 鼓楼

beacon tower 烽火台

memorial archway 牌坊

Taoist temple 道观

Buddhist temple 佛教寺庙

Chinese quadrangle/siheyuan 四合院

shikumen 石库门

7. Classical Works 经典著作

The Book of Songs《诗经》

The Analects of Confucius《论语》

Records of the Historian《史记》

History as a Mirror《资治通鉴》

Yellow Emperor's Internal Canon of Medicine/Huangdi Neijing《黄帝内经》

Compendium of Materia Medica《本草纲目》

The Art of War《孙子兵法》

Journey to the West/*The Monkey King*《西游记》

A Dream of Red Mansions/*The Story of the Stone*《红楼梦》

Romance of the Three Kingdoms《三国演义》

Water Margin/*Outlaws of the Marsh*《水浒传》

8. Arts and Crafts 艺术和技艺

Beijing Opera/Peking Opera 京剧

Kunqu Opera 昆曲

facial painting 脸谱

cross talk 相声

shadow play 皮影戏

Tai Chi/tai chi/tai ji 太极

Chinese martial arts/Kung Fu 武术,功夫

chime bells/bianzhong 编钟

Chinese two-stringed fiddle/erhu 二胡

Chinese lute/pipa 琵琶

Chinese zither/guzheng 古筝

Chinese seven-stringed zither/guqin 古琴

Chinese painting 国画

ink wash painting 水墨画

clay figure 泥人

scroll 卷轴

calligraphy 书法

the Four Treasures of the Study 文房四宝

writing brush/painting brush 毛笔

ink stick 墨

rice paper/Xuan paper 宣纸

inkstone 砚

paperweight 镇纸

seal/stamp 印/玺

seal cutting 篆刻

carving 雕刻

porcelain/china 瓷器

blue and white porcelain 青花瓷

cloisonné 景泰蓝

tri-coloured glazed pottery of the Tang Dynasty 唐三彩

Chinese knot 中国结

cheongsam/qipao 旗袍

embroidery 刺绣

Traditional Chinese Medicine 中医

feel the pulse/give a pulse diagnosis 把脉

Chinese herbal medicine 中草药

acupuncture 针灸

cupping therapy 拔罐

tuina 推拿

moxibustion 艾灸

qigong 气功

dietary therapy 食疗

guasha 刮痧

9. the Four Great Inventions 四大发明

printing 印刷术

gunpowder 火药

compass 指南针

papermaking 造纸术

上海市中高职贯通教育英语课程标准开发项目组名单

组　长： 陆勤超　上海市教育委员会教学研究室

组　员：（按姓氏笔画排序）

　　　　　刘　军　上海出版印刷高等专科学校
　　　　　肖　潇　上海电子信息职业技术学院
　　　　　吴文斌　上海市工业技术学校
　　　　　吴江华　上海民航职业技术学院
　　　　　张　蕾　上海电子信息职业技术学院
　　　　　陈文杰　上海工艺美术职业学院
　　　　　范丽迪　上海市工商外国语学校
　　　　　姚晨茁　上海市航空服务学校
　　　　　徐　悦　上海市现代流通学校
　　　　　黄媛媛　上海城建职业学院
　　　　　程艳赟　上海市南湖职业学校
　　　　　谢永业　上海市工商外国语学校

参 考 文 献

[1] Airasian, P. W. Assessment in the classroom: A concise approach[M]. New York: McGraw-Hill, 2000.

[2] Christie, F. Language Education Throughout the School Years: A Functional Perspective[M]. Oxford: Wiley-Blackwell, 2012.

[3] Graves, K. Designing Language Courses: A Guide for Teachers[M]. Boston: Heinle & Heinle, 2000.

[4] Halliday, M. A. k. An Introduction to Functional Grammar (3rd Ed.)[M], London: Hodder Arnold, 2004.

[5] Nation P, J. Macalister. Language Curriculum Design[M]. New York: Routledge, 2010.

[6] Gary, D. Borich. Observation Skills for Effective Teaching[M]. London: Paradigm Publishers, 2014.

[7] Richards, J, C. Curriculum Development in Language Teaching[M]. Cambridge: Cambridge University Press, 2001.

[8] Richards, J. C. Key Issues in Language Teaching[M]. Cambridge: Cambridge University Press, 2015.

[9] 程晓堂.系统功能语言学对设置英语课程目标的启示[J].中国外语教育: 2014(03): 3-11.

[10] 程晓堂.核心素养下的英语教学理念与实践[M].南宁:广州教育出版社,2021.

[11] 陈琦,刘儒德.当代教育心理学[M].北京:北京师范大学出版社,2019.

[12] 何兆熊.新编语用学概要[M].上海：上海外语教育出做社,2000.

[13] 胡德海.教育学原理[M].北京：人民教育出版社,2013.

[14] 黄甫全.现代课程与教学论[M].北京：人民教育出版社,2011.

[15] 教育部考试中心.中国高考评价体系[M].北京：人民教育出版社,2019.

[16] 林崇德.21世纪学生发展核心素养研究[M].北京：北京师范大学出版社,2019.

[17] 刘辉.基于课程标准的教学目标体系：研制规格、路径与过程[J].上海教育科研：2021(01)：5-9.

[18] 刘建达,吴莎.中国英语能力等级量表研究[M].北京：高等教育出版社,2019.

[19] 刘月霞,郭华.深度学习：走向核心素养：理论普及读本[M].北京：教育科学出版社,2018.

[20] 梅德明,王蔷.改什么？如何教？怎样考？高中英语新课标解析[M].北京：外语教学与研究出版社,2018.

[21] 梅德明,王蔷.普通高中英语课程标准(2017年版2020年修订)解读[M].北京：高等教育出版社,2020.

[22] 欧洲理事会文化合作教育委员会.欧洲语言共同参考框架：学习、教学、评估[M].北京：外语教学与研究出版社,2008.

[23] 上海市教育委员会.上海市中等职业学校英语课程标准[M].上海：华东师范大学出版社,2015.

[24] 束定芳,庄智象.现代外语教学：理论、实践与方法[M].上海：上海外语教育出版社,2008.

[25] 文秋芳.二语习得重点问题研究[M].北京：外语教学与研究出版社,2010.

[26] 俞红珍.课程内容、教材内容、教学内容的术语之辨——以英语学科为例[J].课程·教材·教法,2005(08)：52-53.

[27] 余文森.核心素养导向的课堂教学[M].上海：上海教育出版社,2017.

[28] 中华人民共和国教育部.义务教育英语课程标准(2011年版)[S].北京：北京师范大学出版社,2012.

[29] 中华人民共和国教育部.普通高中英语课程标准(2017年版2020年修订)[S].北京：人民教育出版社,2020.

[30] 中华人民共和国教育部.中等职业学校英语课程标准(2020年版)[S].北京：人民教育出版社,2020.

[31] 中华人民共和国教育部.高等职业教育专科英语课程标准(2021年版)[S].北京：人民教育出版社,2021.

[32] 钟启泉.课程论[M].北京：教育科学出版社,2007.

[33] 钟启泉.课堂研究[M].上海：华东师范大学出版社,2016.